TO

FROM

DATE

For My
Mom

For My Mom

Inspirations to Brighten Your Day

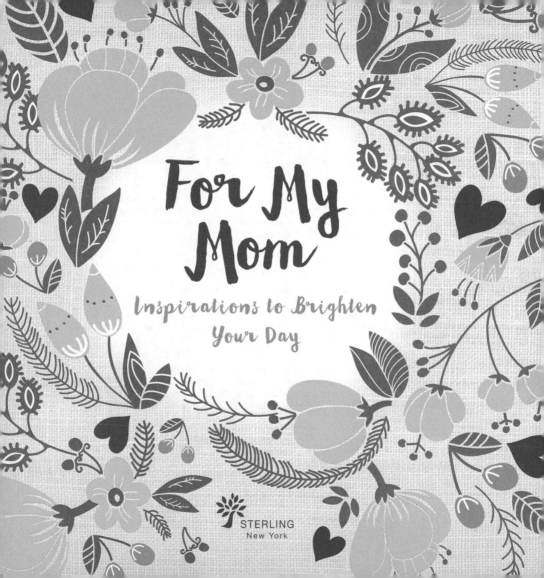

STERLING
New York

STERLING
New York

An Imprint of Sterling Publishing Co., Inc.
1166 Avenue of the Americas
New York, NY 10036

ISBN 978-1-4549-2883-6

Distributed in Canada by Sterling Publishing Co., Inc.

C/o Canadian Manda Group, 664 Annette Street
Toronto, Ontario M6S 2C8, Canada
Distributed in the United Kingdom by GMC Distribution Services
Castle Place, 166 High Street, Lewes, East Sussex BN7 1XU, England
Distributed in Australia by NewSouth Books
45 Beach Street, Coogee NSW 2034, Australia

For information about custom editions, special sales,
and premium and corporate purchases, please
contact Sterling Special Sales at 800-805-5489
or specialsales@sterlingpublishing.com.

Manufactured in Canada

2 4 6 8 10 9 7 5 3 1

sterlingpublishing.com

Compiled by Wafa Tarnowska
Foreword by Adrian Gilbert

"To my mother Najla
and my godmother Ketty,
role models extraordinaire."
—WT

Foreword

THE WORD "MOTHER" CONJURES UP A THOUSAND IMAGES: visions of your mother, the mothers of your friends and relatives, mothers on television and in the movies. For an infant, its relationship with its mother is primal. Although most studies indicate that a newborn is too young to retain conscious memories, many people believe that hazy images of our mothers from the very earliest days of life endure because they are so strong. Our mother is the first person with whom we come into contact, and this often happens long before birth. Our mothers nurture us in utero for nine long months, and afterwards may have even fed us with milk drawn from their own bodies. A mother's heartbeat and the soft lullabies she sings are the most comforting sounds an infant hears in what is an unfamiliar world.

Without motherhood, there can be no future generation to carry on our human story. In many cultures, the primary life-giving deity is seen as a mother: she who gives birth, nurtures, and protects the newborn. From Durga in Hindu cosmology to Tiamat in Babylon to the Virgin Mary of the Bible, there are many representations of strong women bringing life into this world and defending it against all adversity. Because we are conscious beings who think beyond the immediate experience of life to contemplate the larger view, we have transferred the image of Mother from the human world to the universe we see around us. In the greater, cosmological scheme of things, we conjecture a Great Mother of All Things. In alchemy she is the Prima Marteria, the "First Matter" out of which grow all and everything. The Great Mother brings new life to maturity, nurturing it with her own material—this word deriving from the Latin for mother: mater. The creations she nurtures can be on the scale of galaxies, star systems, suns, planets, or moons. At a closer level, the Great Mother becomes Mother Nature, the living, breathing embodiment of all life on Earth. Though we do not see her face directly, we witness her activity in the life-forms all around us, including, of course, ourselves.

Yet "mother" describes a complex relationship that is equal parts power and protection. While the Virgin Mary occupies a central place in the iconography of Christianity as always loving, always nurturing, always pure, and ultimately beyond this sinful world, in other religions and cultures the Great Mother is also the Great Destroyer. We witness this most clearly in the Hindu goddess Kali, whose necklace is made from human skulls and also in the Aztec goddess Coatlique: "the one with the skirt of snakes." Both represent the destructive aspect of nature. For in order for life to be sustained in our material world, there must also be death. Big fish eat little fish, carnivores eat herbivores, and herbivores eat plant life. That is one aspect of Kali/Coatlique but another is the simple dictum: "from dust you have come and to dust you must go." In other words, our lives on planet Earth are finite, but the relationships we nurture here are important and enduring, and some would say that they are imbued with a spark of the Divine.

Known by a thousand names, a mother's love is a place of joy and hope, a gift to us that is worth cherishing throughout our lives.

—Adrian G. Gilbert

New and Young Mothers

A mother's joy begins
when a new life is stirring inside . . .
when a tiny heartbeat is heard for the first time,
and a playful kick reminds her
that she is never alone.

—Anonymous

Ah, let her go, kind Lord, where mothers go
And boast his pretty words and ways, and plan
The proud and happy years that they shall know
Together, when her son is grown a man.

—Dorothy Parker ("Prayer for a New Mother")

My little love, my darling,
You were a doorway to me;
You let me out of the confines
Into this strange countrie,
Where people are crowded like thistles,
Yet are shapely and comely to see.
My little love, my dearest
Twice have you issued me,
Once from your womb, sweet mother,
Once from myself, to be
Free of all hearts, my darling,
Of each heart's home-life free.

—D. H. Lawrence, English Novelist and Poet ("The Virgin Mother")

I love to think that with a wistful wonder
She held her baby warm
against her breast;
That never any fear awoke where under
She shuddered at her gift,
or trembled lest
Thru the great doors of birth
Here to a windy earth
She lured from heaven a
half-unwilling guest.

—Sara Teasdale, American Poet ("The Mother of a Poet")

Where do we learn about love?
It is from our mothers.
They show us the way.
Our understanding
of love begins there.

—Robert Browning, American Poet

And in her heart she heard

His first dim-spoken word—

She only of them all could understand,

Flushing to feel at last

The silence over-past,

Thrilling as though her hand

had touched God's hand.

—Sara Teasdale, American Poet ("The Mother of a Poet")

Seven years childless, marriage past,

A Son, a son is born at last:

So exactly limp'd and fair.

Full of good Spirits, Meen, and Air . . .

—Katherine Philips, Anglo-Welsh Poet ("Epitaph on her Son H. P.")

Being a young mother doesn't mean that my life is over. It simply means that my life starts a little early.

—Anonymous

Then as she longed for it to sleep,
To her surprise
It just relaxed within her keep
With closing eyes.
And as it lay upon her breast
So still its breath,
So exquisite its utter rest
It looked like death.

It seemed like it had slipped away
To shadow land;
With tiny face like tinted clay
And waxen hand.
No ghost of sigh, no living look . . .
Then with an ache
Of panic fear and love she shook
Her babe awake.

—Robert William Service, British Canadian Poet ("Young Mother")

Mother
Earth

Praised be You, my Lord, through our Sister, Mother Earth, who sustains and governs us, producing varied fruits with colored flowers and herbs.

—Saint Francis of Assisi

Everything in nature bespeaks the mother. The sun is the mother of earth and gives it its nourishment of heart; it never leaves the universe at night until it has put the earth to sleep to the song of the sea and the hymn of birds and brooks.

—Khalil Gibran, Lebanese-American Writer and Artist ("The Mother")

O, Mother of the Universe,
those who praise you by the words:
Ambika, Jaganmayi and Maya,
will obtain all.

—Kalika Purana, Hindu Religious Text

And the mother, the prototype of all
existence, is the eternal spirit,
full of beauty and love.

—Khalil Gibran, Lebanese-American Writer and Artist ("The Mother")

First there was the sea, everything was
dark. There was no sun, no moon,
nor people, nor animals, nor plants.
The sea was The Mother. The Mother
was not the people, nor anything. She
was the Spirit of what had come and
She was Awareness and Memory.

—Pre-Colombian Kogi Tribe

O Mother of Imupa, advocate for
the whole [feminine] world! What
a remarkable Mother I have!

O Mother, a pillar, a refuge! O Mother,
to whom all prostrate in greeting

Before one enters Her habitation!
I am justly proud of my Mother.

O Mother who arrives, who arrives
majestic and offers water to all!

—Yoruba Prayer (Nigeria)

The universe, immovable
as well as movable,
is pervaded by the Devi.

She is all that is sacrificed to and
worshipped by the Devas;
And She is all that is food and drink;

Manifold in form and name,
Devi is everywhere—
In trees, in the Earth, in the air,
in the ether, in water, and in fire.

—Devi Purana, Sanskrit Text

Nature the gentlest mother is,
Impatient of no child,
The feeblest of the waywardest.
Her admonition mild.

—Emily Dickinson, American Poet
("Nature the Gentlest Mother Is")

When all the children sleep,
She turns as long away
As will suffice to light her lamps,
Then bending from the sky

With infinite affection
And infiniter care,
Her golden finger on her lip,
Wills silence everywhere.

—Emily Dickinson, American Poet
("Nature the Gentlest Mother Is")

Pensive, on her dead gazing,
I heard the Mother of All,

Desperate, on the torn bodies, on the
forms covering the battle—fields gazing;

(As the last gun ceased—but the scent
of the powder-smoke linger'd;)
As she call'd to her earth with
mournful voice while she stalk'd:

Absorb them well, O my earth,
she cried—I charge you, lose not
my sons! lose not an atom.

—Walt Whitman, American Poet
("Pensive on Her Dead Gazing, I Heard the Mother of All")

And you, mountain sides—and the woods where my dear children's blood, trickling, redden'd;

And you trees, down in your roots, to bequeath to all future trees,

My dead absorb—my young men's beautiful bodies absorb—and their precious, precious, precious blood.

—Walt Whitman, American Poet
("Pensive on Her Dead Gazing, I Heard the Mother of All")

No more such! . . .
My species are dwindling,
My forests grow barren,
My popinjays fail from their tappings,
My larks from their strain.

My leopardine beauties are rarer,
My tusky ones vanish,
My children have aped mine own slaughters
To quicken my wane.

—Thomas Hardy, English Novelist and Poet ("The Mother Mourns")

Because we are her fields of corn;
Because our fires are all reborn
From her bosom's deathless embers,
Flaming
As she remembers
The springtime
And Virginia,
Our Mother, Pocahontas.
She sings of lilacs, maples, wheat,
Her own soil sings beneath her feet,
Of springtime
And Virginia,
Our Mother, Pocahontas.

—Nicholas Vachel Lindsay, American Poet ("Our Mother Pocahontas")

Mother of all the high-strung poets
and singers departed,

Mother of all the grass that weaves over
their graves the glory of the field,

Mother of all the manifold forms of life,
deep-bosomed, patient, impassive,

Silent brooder and nurse of lyrical joys and sorrows!

Out of thee, yea, surely out of the fertile depth below thy breast,

Issued in some strange way,
thou lying motionless, voiceless,

All these songs of nature, rhythmical,
passionate, yearning,

Coming in music from earth,
but not unto earth returning.

—Henry Van Dyke Jr., American Author ("Mother Earth")

All of thy flowers and birds and
forests and flowing waters

Are but enchanted forms to
embody the life of the spirit;

Thou thyself, earth-mother, in
mountain and meadow and ocean,

Holdest the poem of God,
eternal thought and emotion.

—Henry Van Dyke Jr., American Author ("Mother Earth")

My son, too old is the Earth
don't make fun of it.

—Bengali Proverb

Nature is the mother
and the habitat of man,
even if sometimes a stepmother
and an unfriendly home.

—John Dewey, American Philosopher
("Nature is the Mother and the Habitat of Man")

In Spring, everything is full of promise. . . . The child sporting upon the lawn, and the season, sympathize together, and nature rejoices in her virgin loveliness.

—Charles Lanman, American Writer and Explorer (*The Dying Year*)

And the Spring arose on the garden fair,

Like the Spirit of Love felt everywhere;

And each flower and herb

on Earth's dark breast

rose from the dreams of

its wintry rest.

—Percy Bysshe Shelley, English Romantic Poet ("The Sensitive Plant")

Well I remember, in my boyish days,

How deep the feeling, when
my eye looked forth

On Nature, in her loveliness, and storms.

How my heart gladdened,
as the light of spring

Came from the sun, with
zephyrs, and with showers,

Waking the earth to beauty, and the woods

To music, and the atmosphere to blow,

Sweetly and calmly, with its breath of balm.

—James G. Percival, American Poet (*Poetry*)

Oh, Spring is surely coming,

Her couriers fill the air;

Each morn are new arrivals,

Each night her ways prepare;

I scent her fragrant garments,

Her foot is on the stair.

—John Burroughs, American Naturalist and Conservationist
("A March Glee")

Spring has returned.
The Earth is like a child
that knows poems.

—Rainer Maria Rilke, Austrian Poet and Novelist

The great pulsation of nature beats too in my breast, and when I carol aloud, I am answered by a thousand-fold echo. I hear a thousand nightingales. Spring hath sent them to awaken Earth from her morning slumber, and Earth trembles with ecstasy, her flowers are hymns, which she sings in inspiration to the sun . . .

—Heinrich Heine, German Poet (*Travel Pictures*)

For the Summer is coming
to wed the Spring,
And earth on their altar
her wealth shall fling,
And the Heaven's soft odors
and breezes bring,
And the hollow heights and
the depths shall ring
With a wild overgushing of gladdening...

—J. J. Britton, English Poet ("March")

A day comes in the springtime
When Earth puts forth her powers,
Casts off the bonds of winter
And lights him hence with flowers . . .

—Dora Read Goodale, American Poet ("The Chorus")

Comes happy Spring, like a maiden fair,

Quickly breathing the odorous air,

With grass-green robes,
and round her hair

Apple and almond blooms, with care

Twisted and twined in a circlet rare . . .

And wherever she passes,
morn or night,

All the broad earth smiles
a smile of delight.

—J. J. Britton, English Poet ("Epithalamium")

Hundreds of dewdrops to greet the dawn,
Hundreds of bees in the purple clover,
Hundreds of butterflies on the lawn,
But only one mother the wide world over.

—George Cooper, American Lyricist ("Only One")

And when she sees the deeper suns
That usher in the happy May,
She sighs to think her time is past,
And weeps because she cannot stay;
So leaves her tears upon the grass,
And turns her face and glides away.

—Hannah R. Hudson, American Poet ("April")

However much you knock at nature's door, she will never answer you in comprehensible words.

—Ivan Turgenev, Russian Novelist and Playwright (*On the Eve*)

Everything on earth [is beautiful],
everything—except what we ourselves think
and do when we forget the higher purposes
of life and our own human dignity.

—Anton Chekhov, Russian Doctor and Playwright

Who are you, Nature?
I live in you;
for fifty years I have been seeking you,
and I have not found you yet.

—Voltaire, French Writer and Philosopher ("Nature")

All things belonging to the earth will never change—
the leaf, the blade, the flower, the wind that cries and
sleeps and wakes again, the trees whose stiff arms clash
and tremble in the dark, and the dust of lovers long
since buried in the earth—all things proceeding from the
earth to seasons, all things that lapse and change and
come again upon the earth—these things will always
be the same, for they come up from the earth that
never changes, they go back into the earth that lasts
forever. Only the earth endures, but it endures forever.

—Thomas Wolfe, American Novelist (*You Can't Go Home Again*)

. . . the dark ancestral cave, the womb from which mankind emerged into the light, forever pulls one back—but . . . you can't go home again . . . you can't go . . . back home to the escapes of Time and Memory. You Can't Go Home Again.

—Thomas Wolfe, American Novelist (*You Can't Go Home Again*)

I will go back to the great sweet mother,
Mother and lover of men, the sea
I will go down to her, I and no other,
Close with her, kiss her and mix her with me.

—Algernon Charles Swinburne, English Poet ("The Triumph of Time")

A woman has two smiles that an angel might envy, the smile that accepts a lover before words are uttered, and the smile that lights on the first-born babe, and assures it of a mother's love.

—Thomas C. Haliburton, Nova Scotian Politician and Author

Memories of Mothers

When you come home I'll not be round

To welcome you.

They'll take you to a grassy mound

So neat and new;

Where I'll be sleeping—O so sound!

The ages through.

I'll not be round to broom the hearth,

To feed the chicks;

And in the wee room of your birth.

Your bed to fix;

Rose room that knew your baby mirth

Your tiny tricks.

Bird, bee and bloom, they'll greet you all

With scented sound;

Yet though the joy of your footfall

Will thrill the ground

Your mother with her old grey shawl—

Will not be round.

—Robert William Service, British Canadian Poet ("Sailor Son")

I just had learned to know her worth,
My Father's second choice to bless;
When God removed her from the earth,
And plunged us all in deep distress.
—Susanna Moodie, British Canadian Poet ("The Step-Mother")

And I arose as from the dead,
A life for her dear life was given;
The angel who had watched my bed
Had vanished into Heaven!
—Susanna Moodie, British Canadian Poet ("The Step-Mother")

He who loses his mother loses
a pure soul who blesses
and guards him constantly.

—Khalil Giban, Lebanese-American Writer and Artist

When the mother dies the
father becomes an uncle.

—Indian Proverb

Sorrow for the death of a father
lasts six months;
sorrow for a mother, a year;
sorrow for a wife, until another wife;
sorrow for a son,
forever.

—Indian Proverb—

I do not think of you lying in the wet clay
Of a Monaghan graveyard; I see
You walking down a lane among the poplars
On your way to the station, or happily
Going to second Mass on a summer Sunday—
You meet me and you say:
"Don't forget to see about the cattle—"
Among your earthiest words the angels stray.

—Patrick Kavanagh, Irish Poet ("In Memory of My Mother")

O you are not lying in the wet clay,
For it is a harvest evening now and we
Are piling up the ricks against the moonlight
And you smile up at us—eternally.

—Patrick Kavanagh, Irish Poet ("In Memory of My Mother")

Because I feel that, in
the Heavens above,
The angels, whispering
to one another,
Can find, among their
burning terms of love,
None so devotional
as that of Mother.

—Edgar Allan Poe, American Short Story Writer and Poet ("To My Mother")

Reg wished me to go with him to the field,
I paused because I did not want to go;
But in her quiet way she made me yield
Reluctantly, for she was breathing low.
Her hand she slowly lifted from her lap
And, smiling sadly in the old sweet way,
She pointed to the nail where hung my cap.
Her eyes said: I shall last another day.

—Claude McKay, Jamaican Writer and Poet ("My Mother")

But scarcely had we reached
the distant place,

When o'er the hills we heard
a faint bell ringing;

A boy came running up
with frightened face;

We knew the fatal news
that he was bringing.

I heard him listlessly, without a moan,

Although the only one I loved was gone.

—Claude McKay, Jamaican Writer and Poet ("My Mother")

When my mother died
I was very young,
And my father sold me
while yet my tongue
Could scarcely cry "Weep!
weep! weep! weep!"
So your chimneys I sweep,
and in soot I sleep.

—William Blake, English Poet and Painter ("The Chimney Sweeper")

I kiss you good-bye,
my dearest,

It is finished between us here.

Oh, if I were calm as you are,

Sweet and still on your bier!

O God, if I had not to leave you

Alone, my dear!

—D. H. Lawrence, English Novelist and Poet ("The Virgin Mother")

Let the last word be uttered,

Oh grant the farewell is said!

Spare me the strength
to leave you

Now you are dead.

I must go, but my soul
lies helpless

Beside your bed.

—D. H. Lawrence, English Novelist and Poet ("The Virgin Mother")

Old Mother Laidinwool had nigh
twelve months been dead.

She heard the hops was doing well,
an' so popped up her head

For said she: "The lads I've picked
with when I was young and fair,

They're bound to be at hopping and
I'm bound to meet 'em there!"

Let me up and go
Back to the work I know, Lord!
Back to the work I know, Lord!

For it is dark where I lie
down, My Lord!

An' it's dark where I lie down!

Old Mother Laidinwool, she
gives her bones a shake,

An' trotted down the churchyard-
path as fast as she could make.

She met the Parson walking, but she says
to him, says she: Oh, don't let no one
trouble for a poor old ghost like me!

—Rudyard Kipling, English Writer and Poet ("O Mother Laidinwool")

O flesh of mine,

And mine own blood and
bone, the very wine

Of my aged heart, I see thy dear eyes shine!

I hear thy tread;
thy light, loved footsteps run

Along the way, eager for that "Well done!"

We'll weep and kiss to thee, my soldier son!

—Isabella Valancy Crawford, Canadian Poet ("His Mother")

On the fourth day her son followed
her remains to the grave.

And during the burial service he
most manfully did behave,

And when the body was laid in the
grave, from tears he could not refrain,

But instantly fled from that desolated
place, and never returned again.

—William Topaz McGonagall, Scottish Poet
("The Nithsdale Widow and Her Son")

The mother who lay in the grave, was the mother of my infancy; the little creature in her arms, was myself, as I had once been, hushed for ever on her bosom.

—Charles Dickens, British Author (*David Copperfield*)

I miss thee, my Mother! Thy image is still The deepest impressed on my heart.

—Eliza Cook, English Author and Poet ("I Miss Thee, My Mother")

Physician art thou?—one, all eyes,
Philosopher!--a fingering slave,
One that would peep and botanize
Upon his mother's grave?

—William Wordsworth, English Poet ("A Poet's Epitaph")

World
Mothers

Since God could not be everywhere
he created mothers.

—Jewish Proverb

Honor thy father and thy mother:
that thy days may be long upon the land
which the Lord thy God giveth thee.

—Exodus 20:12

Gilbert put his arm about them. "Oh, you mothers!" he said. "You mothers! God knew what He was about when He made you."

—Lucy Maud Montgomery, Canadian Novelist and Poet
(*Anne's House of Dreams*)

When Jesus saw his mother there, and the disciple whom he loved standing nearby, he said to his mother, "Dear woman, here is your son," and to the disciple, "Here is your mother." From that time on, this disciple took her into his home.

—John 19:26–27

Karma is the mother and karma is the father.

—Burmese Proverb

Eternal, unquestioning self—surrender
to Mother alone can give us peace.
Love Her for Herself, without fear or favor.
Love Her because you are Her child.

—Swami Vivekananda ("The Worship of a Divine Mother")

I arose a mother in Israel.

—Judges 5:7

He maketh the barren woman to keep house:
and to be a joyful mother of children.

—Psalm 113:9

A mother is clothed with strength and dignity, laughs without fear of the future. When she speaks, her words are wise and she gives instructions with kindness.

—Proverbs 31:28

Every manifestation of power in the universe is "Mother." She is life, She is intelligence, She is Love. She is in the universe yet separate from it.

—Swami Vivekananda, Indian Hindu Monk
(*The Complete Works of Swami Vivekananda*, Volume 7)

Just as a mother would protect her only child with her life, even so let one cultivate a boundless love towards all beings.

—The Buddha

The real religion of the world comes from women much more than from men—from mothers most of all, who carry the key of our souls in their bosoms.

—Oliver Wendell Holmes, American Poet and Physician

Adam named his wife
Eve, because she would
become the mother
of all the living.

—Genesis 3:20

Each of you must respect his mother and father, and you must observe my Sabbaths. I am the Lord your God.

—Leviticus 19:3

The mother is the ideal of love; she rules the family, she possesses the family.

—Swami Vivekananda, Indian Hindu Monk

These children of
my soul I keep

Where scarce a mortal
man may see,

Yet not unconsecrated,
dear friend,

Baptismal rites they
claim of thee.

—Julia Ward Howe, American Poet and Abolitionist ("Mother Mind")

Honor thy father and thy mother,
as the Lord your God has commanded you,
so that you may live long and that it
may go well with you in the land the
Lord your God is giving you.

—Deuteronomy 5:16

An ounce of mother is worth
a pound of priest.

—Spanish Proverb

Respect the womb that bore you.

—The Quran

Therefore shall a man leave his father
and his mother, and shall cleave unto his
wife, and they shall be one flesh.

—Genesis 2:24

A mother is she who can take the
place of all others, but whose
place no one else can take.

—Gaspard Mermillod, Bishop of Lausanne

As a mother comforts her child, so will I comfort
you; and you will be comforted over Jerusalem.

—Isaiah 66:13

A mother is a mother still,
The holiest thing alive.

—Samuel Taylor Coleridge, English Romantic Poet

For you created my inmost being;
you knit me together in my mother's womb.

—Psalm 139:13

Woman behold thy son! . . . Behold thy mother!

—John 19:26

May every tear that has ever fallen from
your tired eyes, on my behalf become
a river for you in Paradise.

—Muslim Proverb

Mary Magdalene beat her breast and sobbed,

The beloved disciple turned to stone,

But where the silent Mother stood, there,

No one glanced and no one
would have dared.

—Anna Akhmatova, Russian Modernist Poet

**We are born of love,
love is our mother.**

—Rumi, Sufi Poet

I would lead you and bring you to my mother's house she who has taught me. I would give you spiced wine to drink, the nectar of my pomegranates.

—Song of Solomon 8:2

A choir of angels glorified the hour,
the vault of heaven was dissolved in fire.
"Father, why hast Thou forsaken me?
Mother, I beg you, do not
weep for me . . ."

—Anna Akhmatova, Russian Modernist Poet

Jesus, good above all other,
Gentle Child, of gentle Mother,
In a stable born our Brother,
Give us grace to persevere.

—Percy Dearmer, English Clergyman and Liturgist
("Jesus Good Above All Other")

Only resting in Mother are we safe.

—Swami Vivekananda, Indian Hindu Monk
(*The Complete Works of Swami Vivekananda*, Volume 8)

She opens her mouth with wisdom; and in her tongue is the law of kindness. She looks well to the ways of her household. And eats not the bread of idleness. Her children arise up, and call her blessed; her husband also, and he praises her.

—Proverbs 31:26–28

Don't poets know it better than others? God can't always be everywhere: and so, invented mothers.

—Sir Edwin Arnold, English Poet and Journalist ("Mothers")

Mother is the name for God in the lips and hearts of little children.

—William Makepiece Thackaray, British Novelist and Author (*Vanity Fair*)

The Father has not saved
the world,
The Son has not saved it,
The Mother shall save it;
The Mother is the Holy Spirit.

—Dmitry Merezhkovsky, Russian Novelist and Philosopher

O God, if that I tremble so to-day,
Bowed with such blessings
that I cannot pray
By speech—a mother prays,
dear Lord, always.

Isabella Valancy Crawford, Canadian Poet ("His Mother")

The position of the mother is the highest in the world, as it is the one place in which to learn and exercise the greatest unselfishness. The love of God is the only love that is higher than a mother's love; all others are lower.

—Swami Vivekananda, Indian Hindu Monk (*Karma Yoga*, Volume 1)

**Once in royal David's city
Stood a lowly cattle-shed
Where a mother laid her baby
In a manger for his bed
Mary was that mother mild,
Jesus Christ her little child.**

—Cecil Frances Alexander, Irish Poet and Hymn Writer
("Once in Royal David's City")

Someone's Mother, huddled there,
Had so sweet a dream;
Seemed the sky was Heaven's stair,
Golden and agleam,
Robed in gown Communion bright,
Singingly she trod
Up and up the stair of light,
And thee was waiting—God.

—Robert William Service, British Canadian Poet ("Someone's Mother")

Motherhood is priced
Of God, at price no man may dare
To lessen or misunderstand.

—Helen Hunt Jackson, American Writer and Activist for Native Americans

O Christ of the five wounds, who
look'dst through the dark
To the face of Thy mother! consider, I pray,
How we common mothers stand desolate, mark,
Whose sons, not being Christs,
die with eyes turned away,
And no last word to say!

—Elizabeth Barrett Browning, Victorian Poet ("Mother and Poet")

The formative period for building character for eternity is in the nursery. The mother is queen of that realm and sways a scepter more potent than that of kings or priests.

—Anonymous

I profess the religion of love
Love is my religion and my faith.
My mother is love
My father is love
My Prophet is Love
My God is Love
I am a child of Love
I have come only to speak of Love.

—Rumi, Sufi Poet

One lamp—thy mother's love—amid the stars

Shall lift its pure flame changeless, and before

The throne of God, burn through eternity—

Holy—as it was lit and lent thee here.

—Nathaniel Parker Willis, American Writer and Poet

The mother is the highest ideal of womanhood in India. When God is worshipped as "other," as Love, the Hindus call it the "right-handed" way, and it leads to spirituality.

—Swami Vivekananda, Indian Hindu Monk
(*The Complete Works of Swami Vivekananda*, Volume 7)

O mother blest,
whom God bestows
On sinners and on just,
What joy, what hope
thou givest those
Who in thy mercy trust.

—Saint Alphonsus, Italian Theologian

In some far fiber of her trembling mind!

—Isabella Valancy Crawford, Canadian Poet ("His Mother")

The mother stands by her child through everything. Wife and children may desert a man, but his mother never.

—Swami Vivekananda, Indian Hindu Monk
(*The Complete Works of Swami Vivekananda*, Volume 8)

To support mother and father, to cherish wife and children, and to be engaged in peaceful occupation, this is the greatest blessing.

—The Buddha

Every midwife knows
that not until a mother's womb
softens from the pain of labor
will a way unfold
and the infant find that opening to be born.
Oh, friend!
There is treasure in your heart,
it is heavy with child.
Listen.

—Rumi, Sufi Poet

The ideal woman in India is the mother, the mother first, and the mother last. The word woman calls up to the mind of the Hindu, motherhood; and God is called Mother.

—Swami Vivekananda, Indian Hindu Monk
(*The Complete Works of Swami Vivekananda*, Volume 6)

*In the Western home,
the wife rules.
In an Indian home,
the mother rules.*

—Swami Vivekananda, Indian Hindu Monk
(*The Complete Works of Swami Vivekananda*, Volume 6)

We can't help being thirsty, moving toward the voice of water. Milk drinkers draw close to the mother. Muslims, Christians, Jews, Buddhists, Hindus, shamans, everyone hears the intelligent sound and moves with thirst to meet it.

—Rumi, Sufi Poet

Love the whole world as a mother loves her only child.

—The Buddha

Wise
Mothers

Why do you look at me, Annie?
you think I am hard and cold;

But all my children have gone
before me, I am so old:

I cannot weep for Willy, nor
can I weep for the rest;

Only at your age, Annie, I could
have wept with the best.

—Alfred Lord Tennyson, Poet Laureate of Great Britain and Ireland
("The Grandmother")

Someone's Mother trails the street

Wrapped in rotted rags;

Broken slippers on her feet

Drearily she drags;

Drifting in the bitter night,

Gnawing gutter bread,

With a face of tallow white,

Listless as the dead.

—Robert William Service, British Canadian Poet ("Someone's Mother")

Your children distant will become,
And wide the gulf will grow;
The lips of loving will be dumb,
The trust you used to know
Will in another's heart repose,
Another's voice will cheer . . .
And you will fondle baby clothes
And brush away a tear.

—Robert William Service, British Canadian Poet ("The Mother")

He hurried away, young heart of
joy, under our Devon sky!

And I watched him go, my beautiful
boy, and a weary woman was I.

For my hair is grey, and his was gold;
he'd the best of his life to live;

And I'd loved him so, and I'm old,
I'm old; and he's all I had to give.

—Robert William Service, British Canadian Poet ("Son")

I rise in the dawn, and I kneel and blow

Till the seed of the fire flicker and glow;

And then I must scrub and bake and sweep

Till stars are beginning to blink and peep;

And the young lie long and dream in their bed

Of the matching of ribbons for bosom and head,

And their day goes over in idleness,

And they sigh if the wind but lift a tress:

While I must work because I am old,

And the seed of the fire gets feeble and cold.

—William Butler Yeats, Irish Poet ("The Song of the Old Mother")

For Peace must be bought with
blood and tears, and the boys
of our hearts must pay;
And so in our joy
of the after-years,
let us bless them every day.

—Robert William Service, British Canadian Poet ("Son")

Grandmothers

When the grandmothers speak,
the earth will be healed.

—Hopi Proverb

A house needs a grandma in it.

—Louisa May Alcott, American Novelist

Grandmas are moms with lots of frosting.

—Anonymous

There's no place like home
except Grandma's.

—Anonymous

Grandmother—a
wonderful mother
with lots of practice.

—Anonymous

A grandmother is a remarkable woman. She's a wonderful combination of warmth and kindness, laughter and love. She overlooks our faults, encourages our dreams, and praises our every success.

—Anonymous

Grandmother-grandchild
relationships are simple.
Grandmas are short on criticism
and long on love.

—Anonymous

A grandparent is old on the outside
but young on the inside.

—Anonymous

If nothing is going well,
call your grandmother.

—Italian Proverb

Uncles and aunts, and cousins, are all very well, and fathers and mothers are not to be despised; but a grandmother, at holiday time, is worth them all.

—Fanny Fern, American Newspaper Columnist

A grandmother is a little bit parent, a little bit teacher, and a little bit best friend.

—Anonymous

What happens at Nana's
. . . stays at Nana's.

—Anonymous

Sadly, some folks want others to feel their pain, to hurt as much as they do—or more. My grandmother once told me to avoid colds and angry people whenever I could. It's sound advice.

—Walter Anderson, American Painter

It's such a grand thing to be a mother of a mother—that's why the world calls her grandmother.

—Anonymous

A garden of love grows in a grandmother's heart.

—Anonymous

Grandmas hold our tiny hands for just a little while . . . but our hearts forever.

—Anonymous

Grandma serves kisses, counsel, and cookies daily.

—Anonymous

Just when a mother thinks her work is done she becomes a grandmother.

—Pakistani Proverb

Grandchildren don't make a man feel old; it's the knowledge that he's married to a grandmother.

—G. Norman Collie, British Scientist and Explorer

A grandmother's name is little less in love
than is the doting title of a mother.

—William Shakespeare, English Playwright and Poet

It is as grandmothers that our mothers
come into the fullness of their grace.
When a man's mother holds his child in her
gladden arms he is aware of the roundness of
life's cycle; of the mystic harmony of life's ways.

—Christopher Morley, American Journalist and Poet

Grandmothers are just "antique" little girls.

—Anonymous

Grandmothers are the people who take delight in hearing babies breathing into the telephone.

—Anonymous

Grandmothers and roses are much the same. Each are God's masterpieces with different names.

—Anonymous

Grandmother . . .
Has ears that truly listen
Arms that always hold
Love that's never ending
And a heart that's made of gold.

—Anonymous

A grandma is someone who plays a special part in all the treasured memories we hold within our heart.

—Anonymous

If becoming a grandmother was only a matter of choice, I should advise every one of you straight away to become one. There is no fun for old people like it!

—Hannah Whithall Smith, American Author Active in the Women's Suffrage Movement

No cowboy was ever faster on the draw than a grandparent pulling a baby picture out of a wallet.

—Anonymous

A grandmother is a babysitter
who watches the kids
instead of the television.

—Anonymous

**More precious than our children are
the children of our children.**

—Egyptian Proverb

Grandmas don't just say "that's nice," they
reel back and roll their eyes and throw
up their hands and smile. You get your
money's worth out of grandmas.

—Anonymous

The struggle of our grandmothers to make a pie better than the neighbours kept their brains working and made their opinions much more interesting than those of the women who have their pies sent in from the chain store on the corner.

—G. K. Chesterton, English Poet and Philosopher

I consider the happiness of being
a grandmother much overrated.
How it can make any woman of
experience happy to stand to see her
sons and daughters mismanage their
children, I have yet to understand.

—Mrs. Henry de la Pasture, English Novelist and Children's Writer

The chief occupation of a
grandmother's first year is
to keep her hands off.

—Esther Mary Ogden Sturgis, English Novelist, Dramatist,
and Children's Writer (*Random Reflections of a Grandmother*)

Grandmothers make the world . . . a little softer, a little kinder, a little warmer.

—Anonymous

If you would civilize a man, begin with his grandmother.

—Victor Hugo, French Writer and Poet

Perfect love sometimes does not come till the first grandchild.

—Welsh Proverb

Between the earth and sky
above, nothing can match
a grandmother's love.
—Anonymous

❋

A grandma's heart is a
patchwork of love.
—Anonymous

Once upon a time there lived in a certain village a little country girl, the prettiest creature who was ever seen. Her mother was excessively fond of her; and her grandmother doted on her still more. This good woman had a little red riding hood made for her. It suited the girl so extremely well that everybody called her Little Red Riding Hood.

One day her mother, having made some cakes, said to her, "Go, my dear, and see how your grandmother is doing, for I hear she has been very ill. Take her a cake, and this little pot of butter."

Little Red Riding Hood set out immediately to go to her grandmother, who lived in another village.

"Who's there?"

"Your grandchild, Little Red Riding Hood,"
replied the wolf, counterfeiting her voice;
"who has brought you a cake and a little
pot of butter sent you by mother."

The good grandmother, who was in bed,
because she was somewhat ill, cried out,
"Pull the bobbin, and the latch will go up."

The wolf pulled the bobbin, and the door opened,
and then he immediately fell upon the good
woman and ate her up in a moment, for it been
more than three days since he had eaten.

—Charles Perrault, French Author ("Little Red Riding Hood")

He then shut the door and got into the grandmother's bed, expecting Little Red Riding Hood, who came some time afterwards and knocked at the door: tap, tap.

Little Red Riding Hood took off her clothes and got into bed. She was greatly amazed to see how her grandmother looked in her nightclothes, and said to her,

"Grandmother, what big arms you have!"

"All the better to hug you with, my dear."

"Grandmother, what big legs you have!"

"All the better to run with, my child."

"Grandmother, what big ears you have!"

"All the better to hear with, my child."

"Grandmother, what big eyes you have!"

"All the better to see with, my child."

"Grandmother, what big teeth you have got!"

"All the better to eat you up with."

And, saying these words, this wicked wolf fell upon Little Red Riding Hood, and ate her all up.

—Charles Perrault, French Author ("Little Red Riding Hood")

"Tell me about her. Does
she look like me?"

"She should, shouldn't she,
you're so many times

Over descended from her. I believe

She does look like you.
Stay the way you are.

The nose is just the same,
and so's the chin—

Making allowance, making
due allowance."

—Robert Frost, American Poet ("The Generations of Men")

"You poor, dear, great, great, great, great Granny!"

"See that you get her greatness right. Don't stint her."

"Yes, it's important, though you think it isn't."

—Robert Frost, American Poet ("The Generations of Men")

The woman named Tomorrow

sits with a hairpin in her teeth

and takes her time and
does her hair the way she wants it

and fastens at last the last braid and coil

and puts the hairpin where it belongs

and turns and drawls: Well, what of it?

My grandmother, Yesterday, is gone.

What of it? Let the dead be dead.

—Carl Sandburg, American Poet
("Four Preludes to Playthings of the Wind")

The north has loved
her; she will be

A grandmother feeding
geese on frosty

Mornings; she will understand
Early snow on the cranberries
Better and better then.

—Carl Sandburg, American Poet ("Helga")

In the middle of our porridge plates

There was a blue butterfly painted

And each morning we tried who
should reach the butterfly first.

Then the Grandmother said:
"Do not eat the poor butterfly."

That made us laugh.

Always she said it and always
it started us laughing.

It seemed such a sweet little joke.

I was certain that one fine morning

The butterfly would fly out of our plates,

Laughing the teeniest laugh in the world,

And perch on the Grandmother's lap.

—Katherine Mansfield, New Zealand Poet ("Butterfly Laughter")

But tell us, my dear, all you see and you hear

In those beautiful lands over there,

Where the Fly-Away Horse
wings his faraway course

With the wee one consigned to his care.

Then grandma will cry

In amazement: "Oh, my!"

And she'll think it could never be so;

And only we two

Shall know it is true—

You and I, little precious! shall know!

—Eugene Field, American Writer and Children's Poet
("The Fly-Away Horse")

Just as the sun was setting
Back of the Western hills
Grandfather stood by the window
Eating the last of his pills.
And Grandmother, by the cupboard,
Knitting, heard him say:
"I ought to have went to the village
To fetch some more pills today."
Then Grandmother snuffled a teardrop
And said. "It is jest like I suz
T' th' parson—Grandfather's liver
Ain't what it used to was."

—Ellis Parker Butler, American Author ("A Pastoral")

Mothers and Daughters

She [Natasha] thought her life was over. But suddenly her love for her mother showed her that the essence of life—love—was still alive in her. Love awoke, and life awoke.

—Leo Tolstoy, Russian Novelist (*War and Peace*)

Mother, I cannot mind my wheel;
My fingers ache, my lips are dry:
O, if you felt the pain I feel!
But O, who ever felt as I?
No longer could I doubt him true—
All other men may use deceit;
He always said my eyes were blue,
And often swore my lips were sweet.

—Walter Savage Landor, English Writer and Poet
("Mother, I Cannot Mind My Wheel")

The azure isle of childhood is paling,
On the deck of ship we stand alone.
It appears, oh mother, to your daughters
You've left an inheritance of woe.

—Marina Tsvetaeva, Russian Poet ("To Mother")

What you say of the pride of giving life to an immortal soul is very fine, dear, but I own I cannot enter into that. I think much more of our being like a cow or a dog at such moments; when our poor nature becomes so very animal and un–ecstatic.

—Queen Victoria in a letter to her daughter Vicky

I think my life began with waking up and loving my mother's face.

—George Eliot, English Victorian Novelist (*Daniel Deronda*)

All women become like their mothers.
That is their tragedy.
No man does. That's his.

—Oscar Wilde, Irish Poet (*The Importance of Being Ernest*)

My mother said the cure for thinking
too much about yourself was helping
somebody who was worse off than you.

—Sylvia Plath, American Poet (*The Bell Jar*)

Mothers and daughters are closest
when daughters become mothers.

—Anonymous

Like mother like daughter.

—English Proverb

**A daughter is God's way of saying:
"I thought you could use
a lifelong friend."**

—Anonymous

Flatter the mother to get the girl.

—Corsican Proverb

My little girl yesterday, my friend today,
my daughter forever.

**Your son is your son until
he marries, but your daughter
is your daughter until you die.**

On the darkest days, when I feel
inadequate, unloved and unworthy,
I remember whose daughter I am
and I straighten my crown.

Sometimes, when I need
a miracle, I look into my
daughter's eyes and realize
I've already created one.

—Anonymous

*My life may not
be a fairy tale
but my daughter
is my princess.*

—Anonymous

Is she not lovely! Oh! when, long ago,

My own dead mother gazed upon my face,

As I stood blushing near in bridal snow,

I had not half her beauty and her grace.

—Henry Timrod, American Poet ("A Mother Gazes Upon Her Daughter")

Bless thee, my daughter! Oh! she is so fair!

Heaven bend above thee with its starriest skies!

And make thee truly all thou dost appear

Unto a lover's and thy mother's eyes!

—Henry Timrod, American Poet ("A Mother Gazes Upon Her Daughter")

Her baby was so full of glee,
And through the day
It laughed and babbled on her knee
In happy play.
It pulled her hair all out of curl
With noisy joy;
So peppy she was glad her girl
Was not a boy.

—Robert William Service, British Canadian Poet ("Young Mother")

A busy mother makes slothful daughters.

—Portuguese Proverb

Mothers, look after your daughters, keep them near you, keep their confidence— that they may be true and faithful.

—Elmina S. Taylor, founding member of the National Council of Women

Good daughters make good mothers.

—Abigail G. Whittlesey, American Educator

What the daughter does, the mother did.

—Jewish Proverb

**A fluent tongue is the only thing
a mother don't like her daughter
to resemble her in.**

—Richard Brinsley Sheridan, Irish playwright

What do girls do who haven't any mothers
to help them through their troubles?

—Louisa May Alcott, American Novelist

**A son is a son till he takes him a wife,
a daughter is a daughter all of her life.**

—Irish Proverb

He that would the daughter win, must
with the mother first begin.

—English Proverb

If you would have a good wife, marry one
who has been a good daughter.

—Thomas Fuller, English Churchman and Historian

A daughter is a mother's gender partner,
her closest ally in the family confederacy,
an extension of herself.

—Anonymous

Daughter am I in my mother's house,
but mistress in my own?

—Rudyard Kipling, English Journalist, Poet, and Novelist

For we think back through our
mothers if we are women.

—Virginia Woolf, English Writer (*A Room of One's Own*)

I want my daughter to grow up to be
a strong woman; I just need to be able
to live with her in the meantime!

—Anonymous

You are loved for the little girl you were,
for the special woman you are, and the
precious daughter you will always be.

—Anonymous

If you flatter the mother, you will embrace the daughter.

—Russian Proverb

Three daughters and their mother,
four devils for the father.

—Spanish Proverb

A silly daughter teaches her
mother how to bear children.

—Ethiopian Proverb

Have a close look at the mother
and then marry her daughter.

—Hungarian Proverb

A girl without a mother is
like a mountain with no paths;
a girl without a father is like a
mountain with no streams.

—Kurdish Proverb

The mother is only really the
mistress of her daughter upon the
condition of continually representing
herself to her as a model of
wisdom and type of perfection.

—Alexandre Dumas

Obedience is the mother of success,
and success the parent of salvation.

—Aeschylus, Greek Tragedian

Do you think your mother and I
should have lived comfortably
so long together, if ever we
had been married? Baggage!

—John Gay, British Dramatist (*The Beggar's Opera*)

A little girl, asked where her home
was, replied, "where mother is."

—Keith L. Brooks, American Writer

I want a girl because I want to bring her up so that she shan't make the mistakes I've made. When I look back upon the girl I was I hate myself. But I never had a chance. I'm going to bring up my daughter so that she's free and can stand on her own feet. I'm not going to bring a child into the world, and love her, and bring her up, just so that some man may want to sleep with her so much that he's willing to provide her with board and lodging for the rest of her life.

—W. Somerset Maugham, British Playwright and Novelist
(*The Painted Veil*)

Superstition is to religion what astrology is to astronomy—the mad daughter of a wise mother. These daughters have too long dominated the earth.

—Voltaire, French Writer and Philosopher

Habits are the daughters of action, but then they nurse their mother, and produce daughters after her image, but far more beautiful and prosperous.

—Jeremy Taylor, English Churchman

No matter how old she may be, sometimes a girl just needs her mom.

—Gaspard Mermillod, Bishop of Lausanne

Be the woman you want your daughter to be.

—Anonymous

By the time a woman realizes
that her mother was right,
she has a daughter who
thinks she's wrong.

—Anonymous

I can't settle for just anything,
my daughter is watching me.

—Anonymous

Life doesn't come with a manual;
it comes with a mother.

—Anonymous

I constantly go between wanting you
to be my baby forever, and being
excited about all of the amazing
things you'll do in this life.

—Anonymous

As is the mother, so is her daughter.

—Ezekiel 16:44

Who ran to help me when I fell,
And would some pretty story tell,
Or kiss the place to make it well?
My Mother.

—Ann and Jane Taylor, English Children's Writers
(*Original Poems for Infant Minds*)

My mother bids me bind my hair
With bands of rosy hue,
Tie up my sleeves with ribbons rare,
And lace my bodice blue.

—Anne Hunter, Scottish Poet ("My Mother Bids Me Bind My Hair")

Younger than she are
happy mothers made.

—William Shakespeare, English Playwright and Poet
(Romeo and Juliet)

O mother, mother, make my bed,

O make it soft and narrow:

Since my love has died
for me today,

I'll die for him tomorrow.

—English Ballad ("Barbara Allen's Cruelty")

Mothers and Sons

James James
Morrison Morrison
Weatherby George Dupree
Took great
Care of his Mother,
Though he was only three.
James James
Said to his Mother
"Mother," he said, said he;
"You must never go down to the end of
the town, if you don't go down with me."

—A. A. Milne, English Children's Writer (*When We Were Very Young*)

My mother bore me in the southern wild,
And I am black, but O my soul is white;
White as an angel is the English child:
But I am black as if bereaved of light.

—William Blake, English Poet ("The Little Black Boy")

Happy is the son whose faith in
his mother remains unchallenged.

—Louisa May Alcott, American Novelist

Mother, give me the sun.

—Henrik Ibsen, Norwegian Dramatist (*Ghosts*)

He remembered his mother's love for him, and
his family's, and his friends', and the enemy's
intention to kill him seemed impossible.

—Leo Tolstoy, Russian Novelist (*War and Peace*)

My mother was fortune,
my father generosity and bounty;
I am joy, son of joy, son of joy, son of joy.

—Rumi, Sufi Poet
("My Mother Was Fortune, My Father Generosity and Fortune")

If I were hanged on the highest hill,

Mother o' mine, O mother o' mine!

I know whose love would follow me still,

Mother o' mine, O mother o' mine!

If I were drowned in the deepest sea,

Mother o' mine, O mother o' mine!

I know whose tears would come down to me,

Mother o' mine, O mother o' mine!

If I were damned of body and soul,

I know whose prayers would make me whole,

Mother o' mine, O mother o' mine!"

—Rudyard Kipling, English Writer and Poet ("Mother O'Mine")

You too, my mother, read my rhymes
For love of unforgotten times,
And you may chance to hear once more
The little feet along the floor.

—Robert Louis Stevenson, Scottish Novelist and Poet ("To My Mother")

Here I lean over you, small son, sleeping

Warm in my arms,

And I con to my heart all
your dew-fresh charms,

As you lie close, close in my hungry hold . . .

Your hair like a miser's dream of gold,

And the white rose of your face far fairer,

Finer, and rarer

Than all the flowers in the
young year's keeping.

—Lucy Maud Montgomery, Canadian Novelist ("The Mother")

Those fine little feet in my
worn hands holden . . .

Where will they tread?

Valleys of shadow or
heights dawn-red?

And those silken fingers,
O, wee, white son,

What valorous deeds shall
by them be done?

—Lucy Maud Montgomery, Canadian Novelist ("The Mother")

Some bitter day you will love another,
To her will bear
Love-gifts and woo her . . . then must I share
You and your tenderness! Now you are mine
From your feet to your hair so golden and fine,
And your crumpled finger-tips . . . mine completely,
Wholly and sweetly;
Mine with kisses deep to smother,
No one so near to you now as your mother!

—Lucy Maud Montgomery, Canadian Novelist ("The Mother")

And so, my love, my mother,
I shall always be true to you;
Twice I am born, my dearest,
To life, and to death, in you;
And this is the life hereafter
Wherein I am true.

—D. H. Lawrence, English Novelist and Poet ("The Virgin Mother")

There has never been, nor will there ever be, anything quite so special as the love between a mother and a son.

—Anonymous

There is an enduring tenderness in
the love of a mother to a son that
transcends all affections of the heart.

—Washington Irving, American Short Story Writer

Son, you'll outgrow my lap
but never my heart.

—Anonymous

Your son will hold your hand for
only a little while, but he will hold
your heart for a lifetime.

—Anonymous

My mother had a great deal of trouble
with me, but I think she enjoyed it.

—Mark Twain, American Writer and Humorist

A mother takes twenty years to
make a man of her boy, and another woman
makes a fool of him in twenty minutes.

—Robert Frost, American Poet

Sons are the anchors of a mother's life.

—Sophocles, Greek Tragedian (*Phaedra*)

My mother was the most beautiful woman I ever saw. All I am I owe to my mother. I attribute all my success in life to the moral, intellectual and physical education I received from her.

—George Washington, First US President

I remember my mother's prayers
and they have always followed me.
They have clung to me all my life.

—Abraham Lincoln, Sixteenth US President

So there's this little boy,
He kinda stole my heart.
He calls me mom.

—Anonymous

Dan clung to her in speechless gratitude, feeling the blessedness of mother love, that divine gift which comforts, purifies, and strengthens all who seek it.

—Louisa May Alcott, American Novelist (*Jo's Boys*)

O! my sister Your son is like how you raised him.

—Arabic Proverb

Men are what their mothers made them.

—Ralph Waldo Emerson, American Poet and Essayist

**All that I am or hope to be
I owe to my mother.**

—Abraham Lincoln, Sixteenth US President

Clever father, clever daughter;
clever mother, clever son.

—Russian Proverb

**A man loves his sweetheart
the most, his wife the best, but
his mother the longest.**

—Irish Proverb

Only a mother can understand
the suffering of a son.

—Arabic Proverb

A good son-in-law is like the acquisition of a new son; a bad one is like the loss of your daughter.

—Jewish Proverb

And when I am tired I'll nestle my head

In the bosom that's soothed me so often,

And the wide-awake stars shall sing, in my stead,

A song which our dreaming shall soften.

—Eugene Field, American "Poet of Childhood" ("Child and Mother")

God made my mother
on an April day,
From sorrow and the
mist along the sea,
Lost birds' and wanderers'
songs and ocean spray,
And the moon loved her
wandering jealously.

—Francis Edward Ledwidge, Irish Poet ("My Mother")

Strange he is, my son, whom I
have awaited like a lover,

Strange to me like a captive in
a foreign country, haunting

The confines and gazing out on
the land where the wind is free.

—D. H. Lawrence, English Novelist and Poet ("Monologue of a Mother")

Forgive me. Some women
bear children in strength,

And bite back the cry of
their pain in self-scorn;

But the birth-pangs of nations
will wring us at length

Into wail such as this—
and we sit on forlorn

When the man-child is born.

—Elizabeth Barrett Browning, Victorian Poet ("Mother and Poet")

The angel of childhood kissed me and
went. I expected another would take
me, and now, my son, O my son,

I must sit awhile and wait,
and never know

The loss of myself, till death comes,
who cannot fail.

—D. H. Lawrence, English Novelist and Poet ("Monologue of a Mother")

I bless the God Who such a mother gave

This poor bird-hearted singer of a day.

—Francis Edward Ledwidge, Irish Poet ("My Mother")

She is a mother pale with fear,

Her boy clings to her side,

And in her kirtle vainly tries

His trembling form to hide.

He is not hers, although she bore

For him a mother's pains;

He is not hers, although her blood

Is coursing through his veins!

—Frances Ellen Watkins Harper, African-American Abolitionist and Poet
("The Slave Mother")

They tear him from her circling arms,

Her last and fond embrace.

Oh! never more may her sad eyes

Gaze on his mournful face.

No marvel, then, these bitter shrieks

Disturb the listening air:

She is a mother, and her heart

Is breaking in despair.

—Frances Ellen Watkins Harper, African-American Abolitionist and Poet
("The Slave Mother")

I had a Son, who many a day
Sailed on the seas, but he is dead;
In Denmark he was cast away:
And I have travelled weary miles to see
If aught which he had owned might still remain for me.

The bird and cage they both were his:
'Twas my Son's bird; and neat and trim
He kept it: many voyages
The singing-bird had gone with him;
When last he sailed, he left the bird behind;
From bodings, as might be, that hung upon his mind.

He to a fellow-lodger's care
Had left it, to be watched and fed,
And pipe its song in safety; there
I found it when my Son was dead;
And now, God help me for my little wit!
I bear it with me, Sir; he took so much delight in it.

—William Wordsworth, English Romantic Poet ("The Sailor's Mother")

Mothers easily become jealous of their sons' friends when they are particularly successful. As a rule, a mother loves herself in her son more than she does the son himself.

—Friedrich Nietzsche, German Philosopher

By all the lads who crossed with me but never crossed again,

By all the prayers their mothers and their sweethearts prayed in vain.

—Anonymous ("Any Soldier to His Son")

What blood's that on thy coat lap?

Son Davie! Son Davie!

What blood's that on thy coat lap?

And the truth come tell to me.

—Andrew Lang, Scottish Poet ("Son Davie! Son Davie!")

So, I went to a famous school,
But holidays were short;
My mother thought me just a fool,
Unfit for games and sport.
For I was fond of books and art,
And hated hound and steed:
Said Mother, "Boy, you break my heart!
You are not of our breed."

Then came the War. The Mater said:

"Thank God, a son I give

To King and Country,"—well, I'm dead

Who would have loved to live.

"For England's sake," said she, "he died.

For that my boy I bore."

And now she talks of me with pride.

A hero of the War.

—Robert William Service, British Canadian Poet ("Spartan Mother")

What wilt thou leave to thy mother dear?
Son Davie! Son Davie!
A fire o' coals to burn her
wi' hearty cheer,
And she'll never get mair o' me.

—Andrew Lang, Scottish Poet ("Son Davie! Son Davie!")

Happiness is not everything and
men have their duties. Mine is to
find my mother, a homeland.

—Albert Camus, French-Algerian Novelist and Philosopher

What with noise, and fear of death,
Waking, and wounds and cold,
They filled the Cup for My Mother's Son
Fuller than it could hold.

They broke his body and his mind
And yet They made him live,
And They asked more of My Mother's Son
Than any man could give.

—Rudyard Kipling, English Writer and Poet ("The Mother's Son")

For I gaze in the fire, and I'm seeing
there a child, and he waves to me;

And I run and I hold him up in the air,
and he laughs and shouts with glee;

A little bundle of love and mirth,
crying: "Come, Mumsie dear!"

Ah me! If he called from the ends of the
earth I know that my heart would hear.

—Robert William Service, British Canadian Poet ("Son")

You already know I desire that
neither Father or Mother shall be
in want of any comfort either in health
or sickness while they live.

—Abraham Lincoln, Sixteenth US President (letter to John D. Johnston)

I shall never forget my mother, for it was
she who planted and nurtured the first
seeds of good within me. She opened
my heart to the lasting impressions
of nature; she awakened my
understanding and extended my horizon
and her percepts exerted an everlasting
influence upon the course of my life.

—Immanuel Kant, German Philosopher

Our most bitter enemies are
our own kith and kin. . . .
Kings have no brothers,
no sons, no mother!

—Honoré de Balzac, French Novelist (*Catherine de Medici Explained*)

The reason I'm in this business, I assume
all performers are—it's "Look at me, Ma!"
It's acceptance, you know—"Look at me,
Ma, look at me, Ma, look at me, Ma."
And if your mother watches,
you'll show off till you're exhausted;
but if your mother goes, Ptshew!

—Lenny Bruce, American Comedian
(*Performing and the Art of Comedy*)

A mother has little love for a son who did not give her pain.

—Venezuelan Proverb

"Oh, mother, mother, mother," the boy groaned, and he longed, as if his heart was breaking, to lay his head on her knee, and look up for comfort to her face, as he had often done in his childish troubles. "Dear, dear mother!" and the tears came at last, raining through his fingers, and taking away that dull stupor of pain from his heart.

—Alice Bradley Haven, American Writer (*All's Not Gold That Glitters*)

And all my mother
came into mine eyes.
And gave me up to tears.

—William Shakespeare, English Playwright and Poet (*Henry V*)

I wish thee all thy mother's graces,
Thy father's fortunes and his places.
I wish thee friends, and one at Court,
Not to build on, but support;
To keep thee, not in doing many
Oppressions, but from suffering any.

—Richard Corbet, English Poet and Prelate

He was my son,

My hope, my comfort . . .

And he could appease God . . .

It seems to me to was
pure even . . .

Every light in him is
extinguished . . .

My heart with him is dead.

—Gaetano Donizetti, Italian Opera Composer
(*Lucrezia Borgia*; Libretto by Felice Romani)

Do you know . . .
That your mother would have
to take you in her arms
and in all weathers
walk the city streets
to earn you
food and clothing,
and to the pitying crowd
stretch out a trembling hand
crying, "Listen, listen
to my sad tale.
Charity for an unhappy mother!
Have pity!"

—Giacomo Puccini, Italian Opera Composer
(*Madame Butterfly*; Libretto by John Barbirolli)

And Willy, my eldest-born,
is gone, you say, little Anne?

Ruddy and white, and strong on
his legs, he looks like a man.

And Willy's wife has written:
she never was over-wise,

Never the wife for Willy:
he wouldn't take my advice.

—Alfred Lord Tennyson, Poet Laureate of Great Britain and Ireland
during Queen Victoria's reign ("The Grandmother")

Willy, my beauty, my eldest-born,
the flower of the flock;

Never a man could fling him:
for Willy stood like a rock.

"Here's a leg for a babe of a week!"
says doctor; and he would be bound,

There was not his like that year
in twenty parishes round.

—Alfred Lord Tennyson, Poet Laureate of Great Britain and Ireland
during Queen Victoria's reign ("The Grandmother)"

So Willy has gone, my beauty,
my eldest-born, my flower;

But how can I weep for Willy,
he has but gone for an hour,

Gone for a minute, my son, from
this room into the next;

I, too, shall go in a minute.
What time have I to be vext?

—Alfred Lord Tennyson, Poet Laureate of Great Britain and Ireland
during Queen Victoria's reign ("The Grandmother")

Brother, even by
our mother's dust,
I charge you,
Do not betray me to
your mirth or hate.

—John Ford, English Dramatist ('*Tis a Pity She's a Whore*)

The writer's only responsibility is to his art.

He will be completely ruthless if he is a good one.

He has a dream. It anguishes him so much he

must get rid of it. He has no peace until then.

Everything goes by the board . . . If a writer has to

rob his mother, he will not hesitate; "the Ode on a

Grecian Urn" is worth any number of old ladies.

—William Faulkner, American Novelist

Motherhood

When the mother of the race is free, we shall have a better world, by the easy right of birth and by the calm, slow, friendly forces of evolution.

—Charlotte Perkins Gilman, American Author and Feminist
(*Women and Economis*)

Youth fades: love droops, the leaves of friendship fall; a mother's secret hope outlives them all.

—Oliver Wendell Holmes, American Poet and Physician

A mother is a bank where I deposit all my worries and hurts.

—Thomas De Witt Talmage, American Preacher (*No Friend Like Mother*)

Nobody can misunderstand a boy like his own mother. . . . Mothers at present can bring children into the world, but this performance is apt to mark the end of their capacities. They can't even attend to the elementary animal requirements of their offspring. It is quite surprising how many children survive in spite of their mothers.

—Norman Douglas, British Author (*South Wind*)

You'll never look back on life and think: "I've spent too much time with my kids."

—Anonymous

When life gets hard and you feel all alone, remember you mean the world to somebody and that somebody calls you mom.

—Anonymous

The most beautiful word on the lips of mankind is the word "Mother," and the most beautiful call is the call of "My mother." It is a word full of hope and love, a sweet and kind word coming from the depths of the heart.

Khalil Gibran, Lebanese-American Writer and Artist ("The Mother")

Maternal love is altogether above reason; it is a holy passion, in which all others are absorbed and lost. It is a sacred flame on the altar of the heart, which is never quenched.

—Andrew Halliday, Victorian Scottish Journalist ("All the Year Round")

Motherhood: all love begins
and ends there.

—Robert Browning, American Poet

It is the custom of every good mother after her
children are asleep to rummage in their minds
and put things straight for the next morning,
repacking into their proper places the many
articles that have wandered during the day.
If you could keep awake (but of course you
can't) you would see your mother doing this, and
you would find it very interesting to watch her.

—J. M. Barrie, Scottish Novelist (*The Adventures of Peter Pan*)

I think this power of living in your children is one of the sweetest things in the world . . .

—Louisa May Alcott, American Novelist (*Jo's Boys*)

A mother's love for her child is like nothing else in the world. It knows no law, no pity, it dates all things and crushes down remorselessly all that stands in its path.

—Agatha Christie, English Crime Novelist ("The Last Séance")

Whatever else is unsure in this stinking dunghill of a world, a mother's love is not.

—James Joyce, Irish Novelist, Short Story Writer, and Poet
(*A Portrait of the Artist as a Young Man*)

The mother's heart is the child's schoolroom.

—Henry Ward Beecher, US Clergyman

Mama exhorted her children at every
opportunity to "jump at the sun."
We might not land on the sun, but at
least we would get off the ground.

—Zora Neale Hurston, African-American Novelist
(*A Biography of the Spirit*)

**Pride is one of the seven deadly sins; but it cannot be
the pride of a mother in her children, for that is the
compound of two cardinal virtues: faith and hope.**

—Charles Dickens, British Author (*Nicholas Nickleby*)

A mother is not a person to lean on, but a person to make leaning unnecessary.

—Dorothy Canfield Fisher, American Educational Reformer and Social Activist

I think, dearest Uncle, you cannot really wish me to be the "Mamma d'une nombreuse famille," for I think you will see with me the great inconvenience a large family would be to us all, and particularly to the country, independent of the hardship and inconvenience to myself.

—Queen Victoria of Great Britain and Ireland and Empress of India, mother to 9 children

Mom, a title
just above Queen.

—Anonymous

Motherhood is not a competition
to see who has the cleverest kids,
the cleanest house, the healthiest
dinners, nicest clothes, newest cars
or most holidays. Motherhood is
Your journey with Your children.

—Anonymous

There will be so many times you feel like you have failed, but in the eyes, heart and mind of your child, you are super mom.

—Anonymous

Life does not come with a manual, it comes with a mother.

—Anonymous

The mother is everything—she is our consolation in sorrow, our hope in misery, and our strength in weakness. She is the source of love, mercy, sympathy, and forgiveness.

—Khalil Gibran, Lebanese-American Writer and Artist

Necessity may well be called
the mother of invention—
but calamity is the test of integrity.

—Samuel Richardson, British

*My Mom worked way
too hard for me not to be great.*

—Anonymous

The heart of a mother is a
deep abyss at the bottom of which
you will always find foriveness.

—Honoré de Balzac, French Novelist

I was the seed of the coming Free.

I nourished the dream that
nothing could smother

Deep in my breast—the Negro mother.

I had only hope then, but now through you,

Dark ones of today, my dreams
must come true:

All you dark children in the world out there,

Remember my sweat, my pain, my despair.

Remember my years, heavy with sorrow—

And make of those years a
torch for tomorrow.

—Langston Hughes, American Poet and Social Activist
("The Negro Mother")

Your children grow from you apart,
Afar and still afar;
And yet it should rejoice your heart
To see how glad they are;
In school and sport, in work and play,
And last, in wedded bliss
How others claim with joy to-day
The lips you used to kiss.

—Robert W. Service, British Canadian Poet ("The Mother")

**I see the sleeping babe, nestling the breast
of its mother; The sleeping mother and
babe—hush'd, I study them long and long.**

—Walt Whitman, American Poet ("Mother and Babe")

Sleep, sleep, my beloved,
without worry, without fear,
although my soul does not sleep,
although I do not rest.
Sleep, sleep, and in the night
may your whispers be softer
than a leaf of grass,
or the silken fleece of lambs.
May my flesh slumber in you,
my worry, my trembling.
In you, may my eyes close
and my heart sleep.

—Gabriela Mistral, Chilean Poet and Diplomat ("The Sad Mother")

For I shall be a mother with the mothers,
I shall know the mother's anguish like the others,
Present joy must surely start
For the life beneath my heart.

—Nettie Palmer, Australian Poet ("The Mother")

A mother, who is really a mother, is never free.

—Honoré de Balzac, French Novelist
(*Mémoires de Deux Jeunes Mariées [Letters of Two Brides]*)

Art is a fruit that grows in man, like a fruit on
a plant, or a child in its mother's womb.

—Jean Arp, French Artist and Poet

This mania of the mothers of the period,
to be constantly in pursuit of a son-in-law.

—Stendhal, French Novelist (*Armance*)

A mother's happiness is like a beacon, lighting up the future but reflected also on the past in the guise of fond memories.

—Honoré De Balzac, French Novelist

Mothers have as powerful an influence
over the welfare of future generations,
as all other causes combined.

—Sir John Abbott, Canada's Third Prime Minister, Lawyer, and Politician
(*The Mother at Home*)

A mother's hug lasts
long after she lets go.

—Anonymous

**Mothers, aunts, and
sisters scuttled to and
fro, bearing tureens.**

—Dylan Thomas, Welsh Poet (*A Child's Christmas in Wales*)

A mother is one to whom you
hurry when you are troubled.

—Emily Dickinson, American Poet

**No gift to your mother can ever
equal her gift to your life.**

—Anonymous

A mother is the truest friend we have, when trials
heavy and sudden, fall upon us; when adversity takes
the place of prosperity; when friends who rejoice with
us in our sunshine desert us; when trouble thickens
around us, still will she cling to us, and endeavor by
her kind precepts and counsels to dissipate the clouds
of darkness, and cause peace to return to our hearts.

—Washington Irving, American Short Story Writer

**My mother said that I never should
Play with the gypsies in the wood.**

—English Nursery Rhyme

A mother's arms are made of tenderness and children sleep soundly in them.

—Victor Hugo, French Writer and Poet

You can fool some of the people some of the time, but you can't fool mom.

—Anoymous

Being a mother means that your heart is no longer yours; it wanders wherever your children do.

—Anonymous

I can't promise to fix all your problems, but I can promise that you won't have to face them alone. Love Mom.

—Anonymous

For when a child is born, the mother also is born again.

—Gilbert Parker, Canadian Novelist and British Politician
(*Parables of a Province*)

Mother is a name held sacred

By most mortals of the earth;

It means great love and sacrifice

From the very day of birth,

A love that's so full of beauty,

So tender, so very true!

Something, seemingly, from Heaven

That has come to me and you.

There's no love so understanding

And so faithful to the end

As a Mother's love, God bless her!

That to us our Lord did send.

—Gertrude Tooley Buckingham, American Poet ("Mother")

**Nothin' ever seems the same
When Mother goes away!
The sun don't shine so brightly;
The day seems long and gray!
The dishes all get dirty;
There's no one who is gay
And full of fun and laughter
When Mother is away!**

—Gertrude Tooley Buckingham, American Poet
("When Mother Goes Away")

A man's work is from sun to sun, but a mother's work is never done.

—Anonymous

My Mother's hands, so thin and work-worn,

Were loved by me as jewels, rare,

For they had rocked me in my cradle,

And, lovingly, they'd stroked my hair.

They worked for me, both night and morning;

They helped to smooth away my fears,

For never were these dear hands idle;

I think of them with love and tears!

My Mother's hands to me were precious:

I thought their beauty was sublime;

I felt no harm on earth could touch me

If they were near me all the time!

—Gertrude Tooley Buckingham, American Poet ("My Mother's Hands")

No painter's brush, nor poet's pen
In justice to her fame
Has ever reached half high enough
To write a mother's name.

—Anonymous

Woman is the salvation or the destruction of the family. She carries its destiny in the folds of her mantle.

—Henri Frederic Amiel, Swiss Philosopher

Most mothers are instinctive philosophers.

—Harriet Beecher Stowe, American Abolitionist and Author

Nobody knows of the work it makes to keep the home together. Nobody knows of the steps it takes. Nobody knows but mother.

—Anonymous

M is for the million things she gave me,

O means only that she's growing old,

T is for the tears she shed to save me,

H is for her heart of purest gold;

E is for her eyes, with love-light shining,

R means right, and right she'll always be,

Put them all together, they spell "MOTHER"

A word that means the world to me.

—Howard Johnson, American Lyricist

Sleep, my love,
sleep on my heart.
You are with God,
and I'm with my sorrow.
On you shine the rays
of the golden stars . . .
Sleep, my child.

—Giacomo Puccini, Italian Opera Composer
(*Madame Butterfly*; Libretto by John Barbirolli)

Proverbs
About Mothers

A Freudian slip is when you say one thing but mean your mother.

—Anonymous

There is only one pretty child in the world, and every mother has it.

—Chinese Proverb

"What is marriage, mother?"
"Child, it is spinning, having children, making money, and weeping."

—Portuguese Proverb

You can buy everything, except a father and a mother.

—Indian Proverb

Your mother is the bodyguard
of your father.

—African Proverb

There is no mother like
your own mother.

—Bambara Proverb (one of the languages spoken in
Mali, Burkina Faso, and the Ivory Coast)

Mother carry me, and I
tomorrow will carry you.

—Bantu Proverb (language spoken from
Central Africa across to Southern Africa)

A person who cares for their mother is doing the best deed.

—Indonesian Proverb

Friendship reminds us of fathers, love of mothers.

—Malagasy Proverb (Madagascar)

A monkey is a gazelle in the eyes of its mother.

—Arabic Proverb

Who does not obey the parents' word will be taught by the world.

—Estonian Proverb

Mother's love is ever in its spring.

—French Proverb

Mother is a verb not a noun.

—Popular Proverb

The land a man knows
is his mother.

—Spanish Proverb

**When a child is asleep a mother's
attention is on the child's stomach.**

—African Proverb

A mother is a school,
preparing her is like
preparing a good nation.

—Arabic Proverb

Mother sets aside
and the cat eats.

—Corsican Proverb

There are many fathers,
but only one mother.

—Russian Proverb